At Home in

For Ralph

GRETA STODDART

At Home in the Dark

Greta Stoddart

ANVIL PRESS POETRY

Published in 2001
by Anvil Press Poetry Ltd
Neptune House 70 Royal Hill London SE10 8RF

Copyright © Greta Stoddart 2001

ISBN 0 85646 334 5

This book is published
with financial assistance from
The Arts Council of England

A catalogue record for this book
is available from the British Library

The moral rights of the author have been asserted in
accordance with the Copyright, Designs and Patents Act 1988

Designed and set in Monotype Bell by Anvil
Printed and bound in England
by Cromwell Press, Trowbridge, Wiltshire

for Stewart Adlam

ACKNOWLEDGEMENTS

Acknowledgements are due to the editors of the following
publications in which some of these poems first appeared:
*Independent on Sunday, The North, Poetry Review, The Reater,
Times Literary Supplement, Verse.*

'Three Men in a Boat' won first prize in the 1998 Exeter
Poetry Prize and was published in the anthology of that name.

Thanks to Paul Farley for his notes on the manuscript
and to Michael Donaghy for all that his work inspires.

Contents

At Home in the Dark

The Convert

It could be the way some women slip
into minor when they sing their children to sleep,
or those baleful stories night after night
whose soft iambics set the pace for dreams

that ensures a good handful of us
will find ourselves at home in the dark
as if such subtle planting of love or tone
could bloom into a shying from the light.

Take this one here who can't sleep, adrift
in her room, surrounded by her things –
the bed, chair, the empty shoe,
the desk shaky on its heron legs –

cast now in the steel shades of a negative;
and as she looks and learns to pass the time
something in her turns to a book so long
unopened her eyes spring with tears.

Or could it be at the age of four,
that first display that flipped the switch,
the curved black acres, the hard little stars
that made this child no longer care

for the seeable horizon, the bright seasons?
Let's say it was for that one high-arch
perspective that she made the leap
of faith before she'd learnt to walk with reason.

Errand

See that postbox on the hill? It strikes an almost
tragic pose up there where the four roads meet.
In wind and driving rain, in snow and blistered heat,
it stands alone like an old messenger, cursed, struck;
dumb and trusted treasurer of this town's tendered notes,
its severances and dried tears, its good luck.

Dusk. A thin rain. A child with a letter skips
slowly to the box, reaches up, then hesitates
– so a simple act, freeze-framed, hinges at fate –
eyeing her mother's shaky hand, the indifferent Queen,
about to slide forever into the black lip.
The lamps stutter on, the street is lit like a scene.

She's not to know what lay in her hands, what power
if any, she had before she heard the paper's soft
thud that filled her with a sudden sense of loss
as she turned for home, not knowing the reason why,
leaving the letter to its few innocent hours,
nestled among the others, unpilfered, warm and dry.

Allies

I first realised you were not who I'd taken you to be
when I found you sleeping in the middle of a dark afternoon.
Sent home early, ashamed, in tears, I wandered
round the empty house, shambled into your room.
The curtains fell like a shroud around your bed,
around you who never slept, whose job it was to watch over me
but who now lay stirring your own dreams, elsewhere.
Then you opened your eyes – you must've felt my breath –
and looked at me like a patient coming to, resenting
the first face she sees after a deep and bewildering absence.

Then the day your mother died. You lost your tongue
and roamed the house. When you opened doors you saw
us, your children, neither here nor there but somewhere
as tiny figures receding into unlit corners.
We held your life now in our smaller hands
but could no longer touch you without thinking first.
You spent the nights turning her habits into yours:
putting silk you'd never wear to sleep in drawers,
collecting foreign coins your husband forgot to spend,
perfuming rooms with petals that took years to fade.

And the third time, when we were all sent home early.
I didn't know that room had a door till I saw it shut.
The house had tried to seal itself against us,
and even the dog bristled, but my brother, idiot,
never one to listen, listened at the door, then pushed.
I was curious that you came out fully clothed and so quickly,
proud that all you did was zip up your thigh,
flick your hair, look flushed and embarrassingly young.
My sisters stared at the ground, doomed. But me,
I like to think I looked you straight in the eye.

A Hundred Sheep in a Green Field

The way our mother said something
under her breath made us suddenly hush
in the back and not ask why we'd slowed
to barely a crawl or why we were told
to roll up the windows and sit tight
and *Everything's going to be all right.*
Our faces, soon waxy with sweat,

mooned out against the glass as we crept
alongside cars where men, alone
in suits, breathed in and out their own
serene and air-conditioned air.
Slowly, we came upon the scene:
under a big blue sky
the lovely smell of petrol rose

in seething ribbons,
and a woman in a torn summer dress
was dragging her body across the lanes
where bits of toy, car, family
lay like the remains of a picnic
and a man's head lay sleeping on the wheel.
Then I saw beyond this

to a hundred sheep in a green field
eating their cheerless way through the earth,
eating, eating, until in time
I thought, they'll reach the red hot centre
and find themselves falling,
stiff and stupid as tables,
into that burning pit.

The rain started when we crossed the border
and didn't stop once the whole summer.
We had to light fires in every room,
even the sheets smelled of coal.
My sister sat at the window
closing and opening the curtain
onto an empty, shining field.

Arcturus

I hear the polar bear is moving south,
is being drawn to the edges of towns,
the refuse tips, where he pads slowly over
smouldering tyres, sways through purple smoke.

As he closes in, the button eyes
that've had only to squeeze in the dazzle
of snow now jiggle with the thousand lights
of the refineries, slashing lamps in the rain.

Snow-light has vanished, ice-floes gone out like stars.
Nowhere is cold enough and here, even
the darkest corners are a shaded form of light
but the bear's heading for the centre,

for us and where we've gathered to press
our faces against this screen of heat –
no matter that we don't know how
or why, it's enough to watch it burn –

while children hold their fireworks stiffly out,
feel nothing when sparks hit their skin,
and dogs tremble behind locked doors
and birds freeze, bright-eyed, in the bushes.

Some say there'll come a time we have to leave,
flee as once we fled burning cities
and through a zoom lens see Earth turn
in a shroud of scorched and poison wind.

But you, old bear, will be long gone, having spent
your last days pacing the dusty yard,
swinging your head against a concrete wall,
blind to the scraps of fish rotting in the sun.

Pegasus

On the edge of town where the road
rises like a ramp into the sky,
a pony stands in the middle of a field

hoof-deep in mud as if entranced
by something beyond the constant cars.
Nobody has ever seen that pony

out of the field nor the field
without the pony. Nobody has ever
seen it ridden or fed or led

in or out of the field. Some say
they had to build the road around it.
Not that we cared, not me

and Susie O'Flynn, skiving off
into the woods behind school,
Myths for the Young stuffed up our shirts

then in our hands its blue-skied cover,
its *Do Not Remove* emblazoned in red
and never a need to turn the pages –

the book broke open in one place.
And after one long embrace
we'd open our eyes, certain to see it

massive and white and stamping,
its mad steaming head, its wings
erect and twitching in the light.

I don't remember disappointment,
just an empty clearing, the slight
rattle of leaves, the distant cars.

The Fitter

It can take days. *The vision, you see, is vital,*
without it, it's nothing – a soft toy. Pass me
my eyes, pointing to an old biscuit tin.

It's a kind of hunting all over again, with books
open, photos pinned, ready with needle
and glue. They caught the body years ago,
that was the easy part. But he speaks now

of a *soul*. What, for instance, did the creature see?
Moorland, scrub, veld, or sodden jungle,
desert, wood, the same indigo skies?
The man who fits the eyes has never left

his semi in Cardiff, but he's a master of precision,
nothing's too small, or extinct. Recently
though, a slip in concentration perhaps –
an upright grizzly in the Natural History

has the eyes of a man stranded in his front room,
the telly blizzarding, the fire gone dead;
a bison's head looms out of a wall, dazed,
like a woman just woken, sleep crusting her eyes;

and a pair of monkeys stare out from a London window,
like lovers come to the end, at a loss
in front of what has been, what is to come,
deaf to the whirr and gong of the clock on the hour.

His eyes brim at night from all the detail.
There's a tea-towel over the mirror and it takes him a while
to sleep. *Everything's always awake,* he says.

'Magic Eye'

Try loosening your gaze, the man says
as we stand in the street, in front of a picture made
of dots and swirls, squinting, wanting so much
to see the heart, the deep enchanted glade.

Remember, we once could do this
with our eyes half closed, lolling in the grass
could make out da Vinci heads in the clouds,
dragons curled in the curtains' hydrangeas.

You've gone cross-eyed and have become the spectacle.
A crowd gathers, someone calls out
Hope the wind doesn't change! And so do I
as I can see you stuck here, alone,

frozen to attention in the lamp-lit street,
a tide of litter about your feet,
the billow and snap of cagoul, wind
blading your hair – you're turning

famous overnight, a landmark for shoppers
and tourists who'll circle you with the respect
they reserve for statues and madmen.
But how will they know your desire

to close your eyes, your prayer to be restored
to chair, lamp, your book-lined room?
As the Manhattan skyline soars and giant
love hearts pulse in and out of view.

The Night We Stole a Full-Length Mirror

I'd have walked straight past if you hadn't said
Look at the moon and held my head in your hands
and turned it slowly round to face a skip,
its broken skyline of one-legged chair,
ripped out floor, till I saw it moving
– so slow, so bright – across the silver glass.
We stood there for ages, a bit drunk,
staring at the moon hanging there
as if it were for sale and we an old couple
weighing it up but knowing in our hearts
it is beyond us – A cat jumps out
and before we know it we're stealing back to my flat,
the great thing like a masterpiece in our hands,
its surface anxious with knees and knuckles,
the clenched line of your jaw and your lips
kissing the glass over and over with curses.
You lean it so it catches the bed and me,
I nudge it with my toe so it won't hold my head.
Switching off the light my skin turns blue
and when you come in on the scene and we see
ourselves like this we start to move like real
professionals and my head, disowned and free,
watches what our bodies are doing and somewhere
the thought *I can't believe we weren't made for this*
and I can't stop looking even though the ache
in my throat is growing and soon there will be tears
and I can hear you looking and I know what you're
looking at and it doesn't matter but it isn't me.
You left me behind in a bar in Copenhagen St,
the one with the small red lamps and my face hung
a hundred identical times along the stained wall
invoking like some old speaking doll

the dissatisfaction I come back and back to
and there's this really pretty Chinese waitress
you're trying not to look at while I'm talking to you.
Then you get up and I'm left alone so I lift my head to look
at the man who's been staring at me since I walked in.
He's huge and lonely and lifts his glass and nods
and all the women along the wall break into smiles.
Then you're back and whispering *your breasts your breasts*
and your hands are scrambling up the wet stone
of my back and I imagine the lonely man is there
behind the silver screen sipping his drink,
his eyes thick and moist behind the glass;
I know he's waiting to catch my eye but I won't
be seen to know I'm being watched. Not
till it's over and we collapse, all of a sudden
and awkward, and the room becomes itself again,
filling the mirror with its things, our two faces
staring in, calm and dull and self-absorbed.
Then we look at each other and are surprised
as if we weren't expecting to find the other
here and the smile is quick, like a nod slipped in
between two conspirators returned to the world
of daylight, birdsong, the good tug of guilt
before we tilt the mirror up-, sky-, heaven-ward.

Glare

There is no night on a night like this.
Outside stares in through four blank
squares of blue. There is no sound
but the ticking of the golden clock,
its intricate heart minute, locked up.

We long for the night but it won't come.
The old sugary smell of the sun
sleeps in the beams and across the lino
our footprints follow us wherever we go.
Our faces are burning. We are thinking

of the men in white who carried him away,
as the curtains in the street flipped to the wind
with the dull celebratory air of flags
flying for no one knows why.

Even the siren wouldn't cry in that heat.
It glided towards us. We wanted to run,
screaming, clutching loose change but it sailed
slowly past the bleached and the blind
of our neighbourhood and stood outside our door.

We watched the men in white carry him away,
we saw his long-boned fingers trail the asphalt,
graceful and unflinching as if they were dipping
into the clear black vein of water.

Three Men in a Boat

And me. Miles out, bobbing. Thinking of fish.
Isn't it stickleback who go from red to green
then back again when they mate? Or just before they die?

The rods lean off, bending to the tug of the ocean.
No one knows. Not even the waves that pop and slurp,
the bucket at our feet, knocking. Then –

like a gust from nowhere he's up and *Yee-ha!*
swings his line above our heads – I hardly feel it
catch my throat, a graze like the wing of something light,

but then I know I'm hooked, there, in front of the horizon
seeing the little lights come on, steady and shivering,
the great white shell of sky, a tanker stock-still.

The men, red-faced, fussed with knives and engines,
their fingers thick around my throat while I sat and felt
every limb, muscle, nerve

fall like the quiet fate of silk landing
into place. And there, the one in the white shirt –
how odd – one with whom I was simply glad to spend

the nights should be with me now, the very moment I become
extinct, his face so grim, so concerned, the last I see.
There's the bastard! a voice from faraway,

slap on the back, peck on the cheek, the engine steps up
its whine and before I know it we're at the bar, knocking
back the beers, taking turns to tell our story
to the locals in our bad, our broken Spanish.

Greece

Afternoons we have to hide from the heat
where the dog drags his ragged shadow
along the walls. Knives are clean and quiet,
pillows cool, rain remote as tragedy.
In the drawn room as we lie on the verge
of sleep or sex, zapping bad TV,
Chelsea appear and it's like old footage –
men we thought we'd lost forever, a field,
big-dropped Summer rain and the iron
smell of sperm that heaves off a certain shrub.
My heart thumps obscurely at the thought of London
as if of a not quite forgotten lover;
and the old song-swell carries from the pitch
like the approach of a massive storm, or myth.

Alcatraz

Still one hundred and eighty days
to go till New Year's Eve –
in here you count the days like pages
of a large book you can't read –
when the guys on Upper get to see
across the Bay the party lights
strung out like little chokers
while down on Broadway we get pussy:

hell, they say, when you get that smell
they may as well be walking on water,
the way it comes across the night.

We get down on our knees,
pray for the wind to be right.

Switzerland

Such an elaborate co-production
(Italo-Franco-German) for what
is really such a simple tale
involving three plumbers – granted,
all of different shape and size –
and a towering buxom blonde in a slip.

There's nothing else to do.
The flat is luxury, done out in white
from top to bottom except the wall-
to-wall 3-inch pile which is cream.
You can see Lake Geneva
level as a mirror outside the window.

Dressed in overalls and big boots,
two of them have stockings over their heads
but the little one's boss so it's him who gets
to peek through the spy-hole at her,
pink feather duster in hand, bending
over the sofa, her frilly arse.

I get up as late as possible.
There's milky coffee and a *Herald Tribune*
gets delivered. There's a long shower
and me wrapped up in soft white towels.
There's a lover somewhere across two borders
up to his knees in a dirty war.

The door crashes open, she swings round,
they've got her slammed against the fridge,
her big cherry lips going *nein . . . nein . . .*
The stocking heads hold her down,
there's a close-up of the little one's face,
a sound of ripping above the music.

There are children hanging from the trees,
he writes; he won't be home for Christmas.
I lie back on the king-size bed.
The mountains are dark on the other side.
The towel drops open, sunlight pours in,
I spit on my fingers, press rewind.

Convalescence

I've come from a world where there is no taste,
where nothing happens in a small back room
but a chair sitting still and self-possessed.
For days I watched the cold eternal core
of things, heard the pitiful ring of the phone
(only the mirror did what it always does,
showing me a face I don't, will never, know);
and from the radio came voices of people
who live in a place where things matter.

Slowly though, as embers when blown
can reawake, words have come to their senses
and so to my death and how I've seen it
become a close uncomplicated thing.
But now, moving into the sun I want
never not to feel that warm hand
through the kitchen window, nor taste
this fierce fruit needling my jaw
nor see that bird clutch in its beak that straw.

Stepping Out of the Odeon Leicester Square in the Middle of the Afternoon

Everyone's walking in their sleep
and those lovers, entwined, can't mean it.
The beggar's in fancy dress and the rage
of the man on his phone falls sadly flat.

And it hurts, like coming out of church
when day's big bright arch swipes
the gloom and you're caught between
two visions, a creature in the lights.

For an hour or so you'll wander a set –
its laughable ruins and woeful sound,
its extras running amok – and somewhere,
for effect, a clock will chime a wonky key.

But it wears off. Good and evil fade
and the resonant ending begins
to ring trite. You sit and in some soft light
see a barmaid's plain face into beauty;

how an afternoon can slink off to the shade
of a sickroom or shrine, or that room up there
where, behind those curtains, you can imagine
the wrong lovers lie, quietly, shining.

The Blindfold

Once in a room in Blackpool we had to make do
with the grubby band that held aside the curtain.
I perched on the edge of the bed while he
tied the knot once then (ouch) twice
sending me in that pretend dark back
to knicker-wetting games of Blind Man's Buff,
arms flailing down a hall of coats,
seeking ever greater dark in cellars,
deep in wardrobes, cornered in the arms of –

In that brief blindness you are bereft
but alert to the senses left to you
like the game-show hopeful conjuring out of his dark
a sofa, fridge, a week in the sun, or the night nurse
at noon, the nose-job patient counting the days
– all that dreaming under wraps! Even the hostage
inhaling oil-smeared cloth maps the cadence
of road and the condemned in his limbo
interprets every sound through the gauze of memory.

But who wouldn't seize the chance left
open by someone's careless hand as I did
that last dirty weekend when I lied to his
how many fingers? but did at least close my eyes
to lend a kind of authenticity to my guess.
And though I usually craved the not knowing
where or how his touch would next alight
now I could peek, like a thief through a letterbox, at him
still faithful to the rules of a game we'd made up

that I'd just dropped and it struck me then that in all
our time together, my tally of infidelities,
this was the closest I'd come to betrayal;
and when my keeper reached forward I flinched
knowing my time had come to confess, naked
as the day, babbling, and dazzled by the light.

The List

Take it as read then
that I lived and had a list
of men the length of my arm
if you wrote each name
small and neat (very)
like those they strained to fit
on that thin cross on top
of the hill that no one sees
except the man who walks
his dog (I knew him once)
and even he won't stop
unless he's with his wife
who insists on reading every
name before she leans
to stroke the stone as if
she might herself erase
the lines of time and place
but heaven knows it's the wind
up there being salty and strong
that will before long return
the stone to what it was
like the skin on my arm
smooth and clean forgotten.

The Dress

Then it will stand alone and listen to the new silence,
feel the empty air breathe in and out and where it will,
filling old creases, blowing away warm impressions.
Itself again, chaste, regal, as if it had been waiting
for this moment to return to its mannequin form;
delicate husk, untouched, unworn, it can hang now
if it wants, swing its lonely folds behind a door.

In time it might forget the body who lived inside it,
that quick and lovely thing whose eager skin filled
to bursting every curve and seam. It might forget
the first stain, the nips and small tears, the cunning
unravelling of thread that followed as a matter of course before
the final tumble, the fumbling, the cursing and the rip
when it was thrown across the floor to lie, flayed

– perhaps ruined, as it had to be taken away,
laid out beneath an interrogation of lights
where a man in a gown, in a whirl of steam and gas, bowed
his head to the task: to remove the occasion from the dress.
And when it was done he wrapped it up and it shone
from so much attention and loss, its intimate tucks and folds
re-pressed, dry, clean and beautifully stitched up.

Husband

Is not a word I'd ever care to use
for you; oxen-like it drags behind
it others – tillage, tithe, stable, wife.
Yoked beneath a double load of labour
and love, it's stumbled into this century
with so much baggage as if it meant to stay
and see how it pulls short a loose woman
with a band that snags as often as it shines.

You, a farmer's son, are not inclined
to ask too much of words (casually
you shed the names of all the flowering grasses)
but I'm of arty liberal stock – the worst
for seeking meaning that plainly isn't there.
The book says *hus-* 'house' + *buandi* 'inhabiting';
so does he inhabit the house? or is he
the house? The possibilities are endless

and pointing to the same slammed door.
But I'll not hold you to a photo look nor lay you
under a stone of Loving Husband To _____ .
Still, I need you to come to the city tonight,
to this rented room – I'll be up all night
with a stick, a line that's come up clear and blue;
a dot in position to replace that word,
my love, with one that will at least be true.

Threshold

So we agree not to come together
in the eyes of God, or anyone for that matter,
to take this thing into our own hands.
Sometimes, though, a gesture is passed down
without such questioning so for no other
reason than you've seen it done before

you gather me up at the sight of the door
and I cling as if you were saving me
or kicking us through the dust and storm door
into the curtained cool of a homestead
or, grunting and triumphant, through
the midge-veiled mouth of a cave. Instead,

you've brought me to one Midnight Mass,
placed me in a pew at the back where I can stare
at a man coming up the aisle with an old woman,
no bigger than me at nine and a half, in his arms.
She's lost a shoe and a trickle darkens the stone
behind them as they move out and into the night;

then further back to where I'm being lifted
out of a sleep-filled car by a man I take
for my father, breathing from his collar as he carries me
as you do tonight, towards a porch,
its cloudy bulb, where you pause, curse,
hands tied by the dead weight in your arms.

The Bridge Keeper

It should be an angel's task, this picking out
of those who wish to go quietly,
unsung and unseen, leaving not even a note.

Standing on this bridge takes me back
to Pont Royal, that wet November night
with its young woman staring into the black

river, myself behind, frozen, distracted
I must confess, by the exposed nape of her neck
when a passerby appeared to stop in his tracks

a moment, but long enough for us both to consider
her lost. I like to think the best man won
as I heard the splosh, her cry waltzing downriver.

I've never understood that urge to save strangers.
It touches me as when I see you wave
from ferries and flyovers – brief comrades! –

you feel the safety in numbers, as well you should,
like those clubbers emerging arm in arm
into a dawn that's calm and dull and good.

But 4.48 for the one alone and sober
is my 'happy hour', when they seem in the half-
light to be waiting for me to help them over.

These are my true followers, composers of silence
who've forsaken a world turned strange as a word repeated
so often it crows *no sense no sense no sense.*

But just as the moon lights the way for all
deeds I'm there too for the farmer and starlet,
the strapped and sweating youth entering the mall.

Some would have me hooded and in a way I am
the one of whom you say *but I'm sure there was someone else.*
Brrr! the wind's getting up. Look through this gap

in the mesh down at the starry traffic – did you hear
about the poet who plunged through the ice? –
but I'm harping on and that man's been standing there

long enough (and in this perishing cold!)
Watch, how a gentle shove in the small of the back
sends him not kicking, not screaming, out of this world.

Premonition

A leaf lets go in the cold.
It's the only thing in the world
as it dances down like a little dark
skirt. This light, unassuming fall
is the first and the last so it takes its time
for the child watching, open-mouthed.

The child looks into the open mouth
of a well and drinks the iron-cold
air that hangs there. And time
slows for a stone and all the world
listens as the child waits for the fall
taking forever in the mossy dark.

A shot cracks in Eskrigg wood where dark
gathers and out of an open mouth
of sky a tumble of feathers falls,
a plummeting cradle rocking the cold
in its heart as it drops down a world
too fast, unseeing, for the last time.

The child is running to be in time
to catch the bird but now a dark
shadow like a cloud across the world
is chasing him and he opens his mouth
to cry but instead it fills with a cold
taste of blood and metal. Then he falls.

Calm, at last, it's as if when he falls
he'd meant to jump to escape time;
like a dandelion in the cold
air his body is light as the dark
abiding Firth opens its mouth
to catch him for all the world.

But this town has its own world
where mist is the only thing that falls
and where to simple open mouths
spoonfuls of food are lifted, but time's
not kind to those who wait and the dark
bird is winging its way through the cold

and coming to fall into their world
bang on time. Then see in the dark
the luggage, the cold open mouths.

Dungeness

A man in a black shirt kneels in a garden
holding a handful of seed. He looks up.
The sun is humming like a low engine
and all around acres and acres of earth
erupt in sudden tufts of grass
as dry and sparse as sick man's hair.

Sand sieves through the scalp of a doll
whose despised body lies scattered, in bits;
she doesn't know how to die but she's trying.
The little houses sit like accidents,
their windows broken, their doors open,
guarded by gnomes with hurtful smiles.

Orange iron tracks stop one foot short
of the water's edge. The final carriage
has long since tipped itself down
onto the ocean floor where it's turning
into a quiet and complicated home
for the fish who pass unflinchingly by.

On the shore the corpse of a baby
shark lies on its side, one eye
awake and its penis, open, curls
in surprise on its tender white belly.
In the hollows of dunes sofas
sit and wait like patient guests.

And in the garden two black shirts
hang on a line. The man is planting now
and bows his head as he buries the seed
deep and deeper into the earth.
He wonders if he'll touch the sleeve, the collar
or even the lips of his safely dead lover.

At Serfaus Station

We watch the climber scrawl across the snow,
pause, then disappear over the brow
where what is our loss, for all we know,
appears to others as a dot that grows.

We're good together trudging these distant hills,
poles apart when it comes to keeping still

as now, sitting, cornered in this stale room —
but look, here comes your train pulling into sight
and the moment, for me, you step off this platform
for that woman at the window you will alight.

Resolve

As the stalker sets out on the route he knows by heart
and the climber starts to scale the high and blinding snow
so a man will up in the middle of the night and go.

With only a star or radio for company
he finds peace on the road, to be moving at last.
Wipers jauntily clear the screen the better to see

the blackness ahead, and inside a thin hand
lurches round the calm green face of the clock
and a red needle trembles at its constancy.

There are things he meant to say but now at her door he turns
and sees his shadow stretch and stagger up the steps behind him
as if it bore the load of all the miles he'd covered:

the flooded fields, the black-eyed classrooms and mute estates,
all the Kings' Heads and hollow ways, the lit pane
of one who couldn't sleep. And now he's finally here

he doesn't know why or for whom he came, since
like the stalker's prey, this love knows nothing of him
who breaks now like a climber at a scrap of flag in the wind.

The Crossing

The sun was setting as the *Karoa* sailed
into harbour – from the limo I sat
and stared out at the South China sea
flat as peace itself. I was all in.

At the gangplank they pressed me with the usual
– blaze of cameras, name barked out –
so I twirled the cane and walked the walk
and got away with a quick pirouette.

There was a boy outside my cabin with a card.
Seeing the famous signature I took it
as some kind of joke but I had to be sure
so I called up the bursar for the list.

And there he was in a peignoir with Pilou
his pet cricket chirping on his finger.
Flicking it gently back to its cage he turned,
'Charlot, mon hero! Venez tout de suite dans mes bras!'

So we swapped theories of life and art all night
through his interpreter who sat, po-faced:
'Meester Cocteau . . . 'e say you are a poet
of ze sunshine . . . 'e a poet of ze night.'

Next thing I knew it was dawn and his bird-like hands
lay still in his lap, the cage under a towel
was quiet and the linguist snored. No witness then
to our warm embrace, the pledge to meet at noon.

Midday. The deck is damp and grey.
Neither show but at our desks compose
near identical notes of apology
that cross. We pace our rooms.

Next day we're ducking into broom-cupboards,
engrossed in menus, conversations with bores.
At night in our cabins alone we stand
gazing out at the fixed and brilliant stars.

By the time we got to Hong Kong we could handle
a doffing of hats, brief, despairing smiles
but the days grew fierce and hot, the nights froze
and (dear God!) four more to go till Tokyo.

Waving Goodbye to the Elegists

It was only a matter of time before they left.
I stood and watched as they dragged their craft
across the rocks, waded in till their gowns
rose up like plastic bags. I waved and called out
but not one looked round. Their simple raft
laden with bodies tipped as it drifted off
in the evening sun without chart or weather,
rudderless but for a hand or two feathering
the waves. I'd wanted so much to be part
of that crew – great men and women of the past
moment. But I blew it and wait, again, to be rescued.
They'd moored up on account of my distress
signal which I'd been working on for years;
I plied them with drinks and all the food I could spare
and after, when they sat, sated and still, I embarked
on my own sea of stories (the truly heart-
breaking ones made up, of course). Silence
followed, then days of close muttering circles
that opened with weird smiles when I came by.
Eventually they summoned me to say
that, sadly, sadness wasn't enough, that
to be blunt, I wasn't worth my salt
let alone the paper I scribbled on until
I'd suffered True Loss. O tough professionals!
I sat and cried, How long will you go on?
As long as there is death there will be song,
one replied. But soon surely the sheer
weight of memory not to mention the unshed tears
will tip the balance – the raft will subside
like paper on a pond and they'll slide
(all those Ohs!) into the black sea.

A kind of consolation, I suppose, for me
learning to content myself in these shallows
where condoms come nodding up to say Hullo
and cans carry their own inscrutable signs.
But if they pass by again let them find me,
heart intact, hollow Bic in hand,
engraving lines on these margin sands
that soon I'll see erased by moon and tides —
their words come true *Not we but time decides.*

Our Lady

Like a diver come to the end of the board
I stall a moment, hinging at the kerb
as something I'd taken for lost returns:
the image of our lady stood on the corner,
her white plastic coat aglow in the rain,
the way she never smiled or spoke but could
with the raising of one blistered hand
bring to heel those hundreds of men;
how, once she'd paved the way for us
to walk, hand in hand and without fear,
for the seconds it took to cross we felt ourselves
to be centre-stage before the town
who sat stilled and doleful in their seats.
And when we passed we'd glance up
at her chins, gently carved and receding
as she stood surveying her becalmed sea.

Once, swinging the corner I froze – oh!
there she goes waddling away in a blue cape,
unleashing her see-through bonnet to the wind!
leaving me stranded, wild-eyed,
a hand to the prayer bubbling up in my mouth.
It didn't then so what saves me now
when in the dark and blurry wave of a London rush-hour
I can step out and stay, inviolable as in a dream,
treading water between the glittering streams?

Tidings

When I try to pray, more so now with the years,
I find for all my tongue-tied awkwardness
I may as well be five again, fighting tears

as 'Second Glad Angel' in the Christmas play,
corpsing in the spotlight while Mary sat waiting
on a hay bale for tidings that never came.

Now, although I find myself in church,
unhook the hassock and kneel it doesn't feel like it's
for Him or forgiveness that I hang my head but her

or rather her example: the way each week
she'd shoulder the door, her arms spilling flowers,
the hours she'd spend stitching a star or open book.

And when I think of her I end up sprawled
on her morning-room floor – cut glass and roses –
in squares of watery sunlight, playing 'Sorry'.

I'm here again before this cold and lovely face,
the gaze so old it's forgotten what it held
so that now there's nothing and it's like a wave

rears then sweeps me back, leaving me to sit
it out in brightly lit rooms, or blankly stand
as now before this pool of shimmering votives;

listen for her voice to say *Pray* – pull the string
on my cardboard wings – *Blessed art thou among women.*

there are children in the morning

In a big house in the middle of a wood,
little dreamwalker, warm and fuggy with bed

steps carefully down into a hall of giants
who totter, rouged, loud-mouthed with wine

through which she wanders with an unfathomable stare.
She is not with us. She is there where

the long black cloak of a dream is still
retreating, where she's had to turn and feel

her way over the soft heaving boulders
of her sisters, slumber-drugged, towards

and through the golden frames of doors and down
to this – vision on a record sleeve thrown

among the ash and wine, a hair's-breadth away
from the fire – the torso of a woman, naked,

staked in a technicolour sheath of flames,
her wrists iron-cuffed and raised in chains,

her purple airbrushed eyes lifted to heaven
but vaguely as if checking weather.

The child wants to fall into the picture,
fling her arms around the burning figure

but just when you mean to tell her
that you have no love to give her

she'll wake, shivering, wrapped in a sheepskin rug
to a house shrouded in cinereal fog,

the thick breath of sleepers gorged on sleep
and everywhere an awful wrecked peace

(the needle will have flung itself ashore
after the long unwavering night before)

and out of this ruin as if it had been waiting
aeons a blackbird will burst its intoxicated

song of morning (Morning!) on bed-locked ears
and the child will catch the bitter tang of hair

as she gazes at the ash quietly churning,
all that's left of fire, of a woman burning.

La Berceuse

I once had the power to wake and terrify small children
including myself, by finding I was rocking to and fro,
banging my head against the pillow and moaning
sounds my parents learnt to ignore as they sat and dozed,

I like to think, in front of David Attenborough,
that time in the jungle he comes across a chimp,
alone in a bruised clearing, his arms wrapped
like cord around him, rocking on his haunches, whimpering.

Classic runt behaviour, cooed the narration
pining for the arms of a mother grown weary of nursing, or dead.
But I've seen it too in wild prodigal children
hugging the movement like a wound, in men on the edge

of chairs beating the air in bright, stale rooms.
I've seen it in the standard loony in 'B' movies
and bad acting classes, in the bag lady
and men on their knees, bending, as if to drink, from the page.

Now, though rarer, it's enough to alarm a new lover
as I sit bolt upright, my nest of hair.
It's not so much a long story I say *as one
without beginning or end, but it's nothing* but something

like the sway of woman, the shift from side to side
of donkey and swaddled load plodding along the tide,
the swing's slow subsidence when the child is out of sight,
the sleeper on track for Lethe pummelling the night.

Object

Her eyes were fixed on the horizon
when the man beside her broke out,
'Sometimes when I think of the Earth
spinning I have to grab hold
of something – in my case usually
railings, the solid helm of a bar –
once I clung to a parking meter
till it passed, or I was moved on.'
She stared out at the still water
where a chough was wheeling like a demented clock
and turning he took and he held her
fast in his arms till it stopped.

The Whispering Gallery

Pricking palms, groin-ache, soft behind the knees . . .
I seem to have inherited your weakness for heights.

Remember that time, halfway up the turret stairs, you froze
and found you could go neither up nor down, could only,
eventually, be moved by your small daughter's pleas,
her clammy hand that led you step by step back down.

Or that time when, grounded together, we lost the others
to a ride that had their hearts looping the loop and soaring
so that when the carriage poured them out they ran to us,
flushed and open-armed, as if to share their ecstasy.

And later, alone, watching mum and her friend get winched up
in their shaky cradle – how quickly I lost sight of them
in that canopy of legs, how slowly I realised I'd found them
mouth to mouth in a clinch that lasted a full, slow rotation.

Now, entering this cathedral, calm and busy as an airport,
I think of you being led down from those terrible heights,
your heart returning to its metronomic plod. So, it's
head down, step the first step, but wait –

why waste time and sweat in overcoming this fear
when I'm more than happy to sit here and listen
to the recorded call to prayer in seven languages,
see the repairman halt, chisel in hand, his eye hooked

to some high window, the cleaners already on their knees;
think of all the men lying here under stone,
what once might have risen up to that dome
where children are tearing round like small bulls,

stopping to press their mouths to walls to whisper
Can you hear me? Dust winks in the air like daylight stars
and I find myself wishing you this: when your turn comes

let them lower the heights, without spoiling the view,
let it be easy for you with or without a steadying hand
and let your place be safe in heaven as it was on earth.

New and Recent Poetry from Anvil